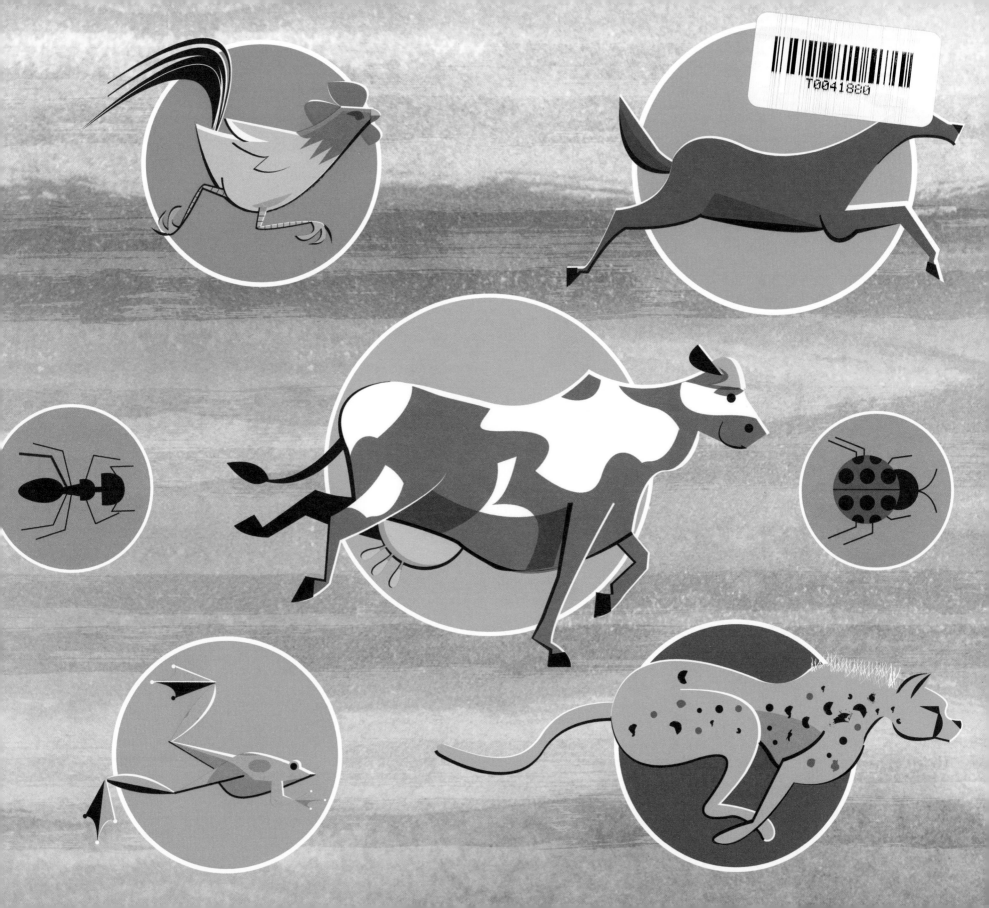

Love Made

written by QUINA ARAGON • illustrated by SCOTTY REIFSNYDER

HARVEST HOUSE PUBLISHERS
EUGENE, OREGON

Cover design by Connie Gabbert Design

Interior design by Left Coast Design

Published in association with William K. Jensen Literary Agency, 119 Bampton Court, Eugene, Oregon 97404.

HARVEST KIDS is a trademark of The Hawkins Children's LLC. Harvest House Publishers, Inc., is the exclusive licensee of the trademark HARVEST KIDS.

Love Made

Copyright © 2019 Quina Aragon

Illustrations © 2019 by Scotty Reifsnyder

Published by Harvest House Publishers

Eugene, Oregon 97408

www.harvesthousepublishers.com

ISBN 978-0-7369-7436-3 (hardcover)

Library of Congress Cataloging-in-Publication Data

Names: Aragon, Quina, author. | Reifsnyder, Scotty, illustrator.
Title: Love made / Quina Aragon ; [illustrations by Scotty Reifsnyder].
Description: Eugene, Oregon : Harvest House Publishers, [2019] | Summary: Illustrations and a simple retelling of the story of Creation ends with a mother's affirmation that her child is the most special person ever made.
Identifiers: LCCN 2018012727 (print) | LCCN 2018019078 (ebook) | ISBN 9780736974370 (ebook) | ISBN 9780736974363 (hardcover)
Subjects: | CYAC: Creation—Fiction. | Christian life—Fiction. | Mother and child—Fiction.
Classification: LCC PZ7.1.A7198 (ebook) | LCC PZ7.1.A7198 Lov 2018 (print) | DDC [E]—dc23
LC record available at https://lccn.loc.gov/2018012727

Printed in China

21 22 23 24 25 26 27 / IM / 10 9 8 7 6 5 4 3

Before God made
the heavens and the earth
He lived in perfect joy.

He delighted in Himself—
One forever-existing, perfect being,
Father, Son, and Spirit
—all One.

There were no trees yet,
no blue sky.

There were no bees yet,
there was no time.

Just God in His glory,
reflecting back beauty on Himself,

the Father enjoying the Son
and the Son right back,

the Spirit rejoicing in it all.
No need for anything,
no lack.

The joy God had within Himself
was so great, so big,

He let it spill over
into what we call creation.

You should have seen it!

In six days He spoke
words that turned into life—

first light,
then sky,
    then earth with fruit trees,
        then sun, moon, and stars,

then birds flying,
fish swimming,

then all the animals that live and crawl on the ground
(all that "Moo!" and all that growl).

And all of it was good,
with it all God was pleased.

But on the sixth day God made
something new,
something unique,
something to rule over the rest—
His greatest art piece.

Something so much like Him,
He called them His image.
And with them, His children,
God was very pleased.

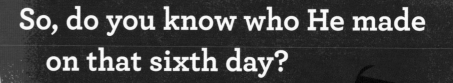

So, do you know who He made on that sixth day?

People!
Like you and like me.

Can you imagine the happiness
God felt to see

all that He made out of love,
not out of need?

The Father loving the Son
and the Son right back,
the Spirit rejoicing in it all.

A perfect love union,
forever intact.

And now all that He made in six days
was an overflow of that:
God's happiness within Himself
bubbled over to make creation,
sharing with them His joy,
allowing them to know and praise Him.

You see, God is Love—
the Father, the Spirit, the Son—
And Love loved so much
that Love made us.
Love caused creation.

And you know what?
Daddy and I know what it's like
to love so much

that something new—
actually, someone new—
became true.

Someone made out of our love,
someone who gets to share our hugs,
someone beautiful
who came to be when we became one.

Someone who reminds us
of God's delight in us.

Do you know who that someone might be?
Made from love between Daddy and me?
Is it a tree? Is it a fruit?
Is it a fish? A bird? A moose?

No, no, no.
None of those things will do.
Our love made someone
so special, so loved...

and that someone. . .

is **YOU!**

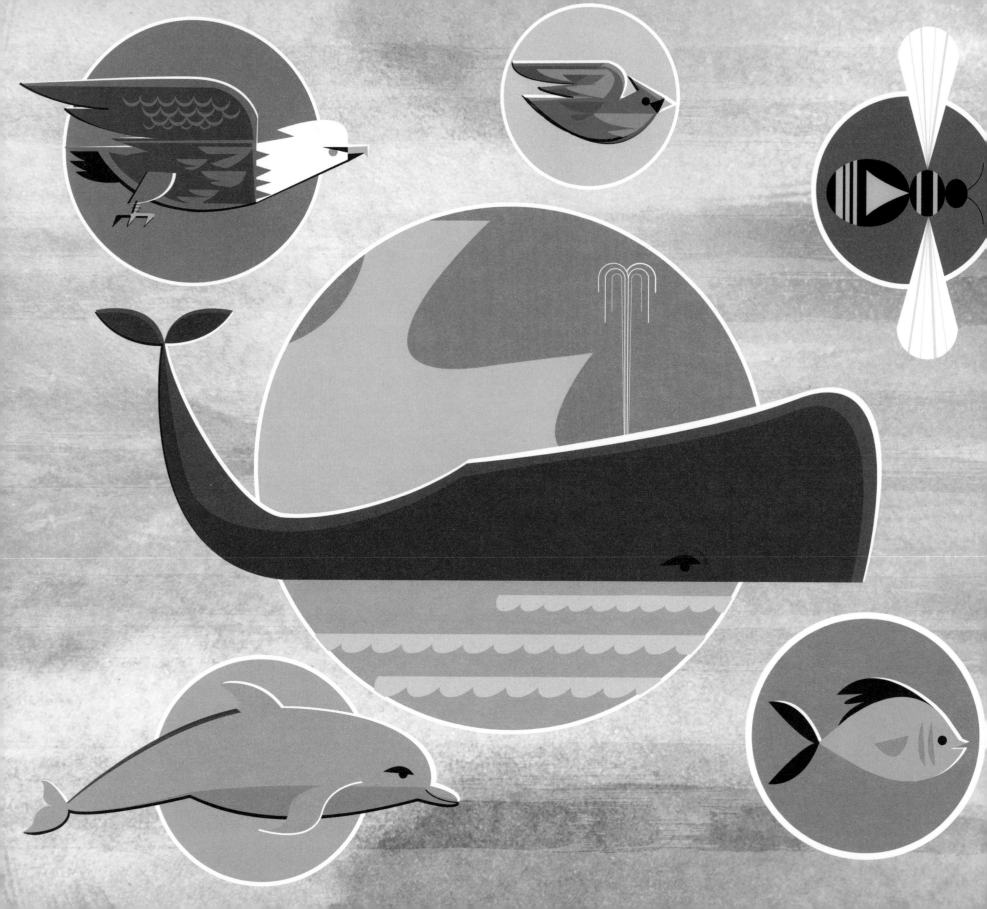